STAGE
2

Arthur Dorros

Follow the Water from Brook to Ocean

HarperCollinsPublishers

for Barbara Fenton

The illustrations in this book were done with pen and ink and watercolors.

The *Let's-Read-and-Find-Out Science* book series was originated by Dr. Franklyn M. Branley, Astronomer Emeritus and former Chairman of the American Museum–Hayden Planetarium, and was formerly co-edited by him and Dr. Roma Gans, Professor Emeritus of Childhood Education, Teachers College, Columbia University. Text and illustrations for each of the books in the series are checked for accuracy by an expert in the relevant field. For more information about Let's-Read-and-Find-Out Science books, write to HarperCollins Children's Books, 195 Broadway, New York, NY 10007, or visit our website at www.harperchildrens.com.

Library of Congress Cataloging-in-Publication Data
Dorros, Arthur.
    Follow the water from brook to ocean / written and illustrated by Arthur Dorros.
        p.   cm. — (Let's-read-and-find-out science book)
    Summary: Explains how water flows from brooks, to streams, to rivers, over waterfalls, through canyons and dams, to eventually reach the ocean.
        ISBN 0-06-021598-4. — ISBN 0-06-021599-2 (lib. bdg.). — ISBN 0-06-445115-1 (pbk.)
        1. Water—Juvenile literature.   [1. Water.]   I. Title.   II. Series.
GB662.3.D67   1991
551.48—dc20   90-1438
                                                                                                          CIP
                                                                                                          AC

14 15 16 SCP 30 29 28 27 26 25 24 23 22

Follow the Water from Brook to Ocean

After the next big rain storm, put your boots on and go outside. Look at the water dripping from your roof. Watch it gush out of the drainpipes.

You can see water flowing down your street too.

Water is always flowing. It trickles in the brook near your house.

Sometimes you see water rushing along in a stream or in a big river.

Water always flows downhill. It flows from high places to low places, just the way you and your skateboard move down a hill.

Sometimes water collects in a low spot in the land—a puddle, a pond, or a lake. The water's downhill journey may end there. Most of the time, though, the water will find a way to keep flowing downhill. Because water flows downhill, it will keep flowing until it can't go any lower. The lowest parts of the earth are the oceans. Water will keep flowing until it reaches an ocean.

Where does the water start? Where does the water in a brook or a stream or a river come from?

The water comes from rain. And it comes from melting snow.

The water from rain and melting snow runs over the ground. Some of it soaks into the ground, and some water is soaked up by trees and other plants. But a lot of the water keeps traveling over the ground, flowing downhill.

The water runs along, flowing over the ground.
Trickles of water flow together to form a brook.

A brook isn't very deep or wide. You could easily
step across a brook to get to the other side.

The brook flows over small stones covered with algae. Algae are tiny plants. They can be green, red, or brown. Green algae make the water look green.

Plop! A frog jumps into the brook.

A salamander wiggles through leafy water plants.

Slap! A trout's tail hits the water.

Lots of creatures live in the moving water.

The brook flows into a stream. Water from many brooks feeds the stream. Some streams are fed by water from springs. Water that soaked into the ground far uphill flows across rock underground. When the water comes to the surface again it bubbles up as a spring.

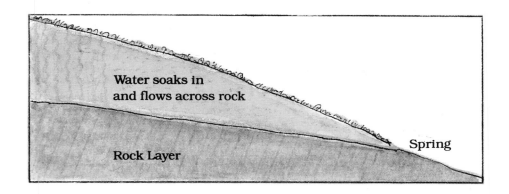

Water soaks in and flows across rock

Rock Layer

Spring

A stream is big enough for a canoe. The water can move fast in a mountain stream! The stream bubbles and roars, racing downhill.

Clunk, thunk. You can hear rocks tumbling underwater. The fast-moving water is powerful. It carries along ground-up rock and soil. Big, heavy rocks get swept along too.

Moving water carves the land. Water and tumbling rock grind the land away. The moving water carves deeper and deeper. Rains fall and wash more rock and soil into the streams. Over many thousands of years, whole mountains can be worn away. This wearing away of the land is called erosion.

Sploosh! An otter slides down the steep bank of the stream.

The stream flows into a river. Many brooks and streams can flow into a river. The river is deep and wide. Big boats can use the river. People can swim in it.

A river flows fast when it runs down steep slopes. Fast-flowing rivers can carve deep canyons in the land. In some places, the Grand Canyon of the Colorado River is eighteen miles wide and a mile deep. The river looks like a thin ribbon at the bottom of the canyon.

When a river comes to a rocky cliff, the water falls over the edge. It's a waterfall!

Some waterfalls drop hundreds of feet. The water sprays up when it hits the ground below. You can smell the river in the air.

A river moves more slowly when it crosses flatter land.

Where a river moves slowly it doesn't carve as deeply. It loops back and forth across the land as it finds the easiest way downhill.

These bends in a river are called meanders.

Some rivers look muddy because of all the soil that has been washed into them. Water from rain and melting snow carries soil from the surrounding land into the river. Valleys are formed over many thousands of years as more and more soil is washed down into the river. There is so much soil in the Missouri River that it is called "the Big Muddy."

Sometimes a river overflows its banks, and it floods. Heavy rains might cause a river to flood. A flood can destroy people's homes and wash away a lot of soil.

People build dams to hold back the water and keep a river from flooding. A dam controls the flow of the water. Some water can be released through the dam so that the river below does not dry up.

The force of the water as it rushes through the dam is used to make electricity.

A lake called a reservoir builds up behind the dam. The water in the reservoir is used to water crops. People swim and sail boats in the reservoir. And they drink and bathe in water that is piped from the reservoir.

Many big cities get their water from reservoirs.

Some people think that rivers and streams are good places to put garbage and other waste. They're not.

Polluted water can kill fish, plants, and animals, and it is dangerous to people too. When the polluted water reaches the ocean, it can also kill the fish and plants that live there.

The river meets the ocean at the river's mouth. The water is still flowing downhill, although it moves very slowly now. It moves so slowly that it cannot carry its load of soil and rock anymore. It drops the soil and rock at the mouth of the river. This can form a delta.

Delta

Mouth

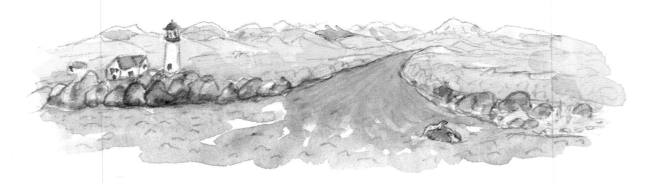

Water may travel over land for thousands of miles before it finally reaches the ocean. The oceans hold most of the earth's water, and cover almost three-quarters of the whole earth.

Many different kinds of fish and animals and plants live in the ocean. Tiny creatures called plankton live in the ocean. They are too small to see without a microscope. Gigantic whales live there too.

The ocean is so big, and so deep, that it has hardly been explored.

The water has reached the end of its downhill trip. Water flowed from a brook, to a stream, to a river. It may have flowed over waterfalls, through canyons and dams.

It was a long journey to the ocean.

The next time you see water in a brook, a
stream, or a river, you will know where it is going.